When people are critical of Christianity, they often assume the reality of something that can't possibly be true. For example, one might wish for God to make this world a better place without interfering in the lives of those who are making it worse. In this book Daniel McCoy exposes five such self-refuting ideas and contrasts them with the realities included in the Bible's message of salvation. He writes in an informal style that's easy to follow and illustrates his points with many anecdotes and illustrations; some of them are funny, some are poignant, but all are relevant. A very helpful book that addresses readers, both Christians and non-Christians, on the level of "real life."

—Dr. Winfried Corduan, Professor Emeritus of Taylor University, author of *Neighboring Faiths and In the Beginning God*

Filled with practical and often amusing examples, this book demonstrates that many of our human desires are not only inevitably unachievable but unreasonable to pursue. It discusses some heavy theological issues in a light-hearted fashion. That's a great mixture, especially for those whose eyes are willing to see more of heaven and its down-to-earth relevance.

—Dr. Richard A. Knopp, Professor of Philosophy & Christian Apologetics and Director of Room For Doubt (www.roomfordoubt.com) at Lincoln Christian University

Certain problematic assumptions about God have become so commonplace that they've actually become conventional wisdom. Daniel McCoy provides a much-needed challenge to these assumptions with logic, gentleness, and humor. As Daniel reminds us, the purpose of the book isn't to shame those who want things that don't exist. Instead, he is calling us to pursue what does exist for our wholeness and liberation. I would say he has accomplished that purpose well.

—Dr. Chad Ragsdale, Professor of New Testament and Hermeneutics and Academic Dean-Elect at Ozark Christian College

# MIRAGE

5 Things People Want from God That Don't Exist

**Daniel J. McCoy**

FOREWORD BY DAVID YOUNG

To Mom and Dad:

*Thanks for teaching me about God and showing that we can trust Him.*

# Contents

# FOREWORD

Legend says that Abraham Lincoln once asked an audience:

"How many legs does a dog have if you count the tail as a leg?"

"Five," they shouted back.

"Not so," Lincoln responded. "The fact that you call the tail a leg does not make it so."

It's true.

Here's the thing about truth. It's real. Truth is solid. It's stubborn. And it's everywhere.

And very real problems arise when we don't want truth to be . . . well, true. "The great enemy of the truth is very often not the lie—deliberate, contrived and dishonest," John F. Kennedy once observed. Rather, the enemy of the truth is "the myth—persistent, persuasive and unrealistic." Carefully crafted myths designed to satiate our desires present themselves as the staunchest enemies of the truth.

"The heart is deceitful above all else," advises the prophet.

This is true.

The heart has its desires. We dare not underestimate their power. These desires account for the bulk of the world's untruths, as we contort ourselves through endless narratives designed to justify self-indulgence. We will do almost anything to banish truth when our desires are at stake. We willfully stupefy ourselves, brazenly lie to ourselves, and comically parody ourselves—hoping the myths of our desire will hide the persistence of truth. And when an old myth ceases to work, we simply craft a new one. It's a cottage industry. "A great deal of intelligence can be invested in ignorance when the need for illusion is deep," opined Nobel laureate Saul Bellow.

And yet, in a world of trickery, myth, illusion, disinformation, and unhinged narrative: there it is. The Truth. Stubborn, but bright. Solid, but clear. Elevated, but inviting.

Always inviting.

When Jesus came announcing that the kingdom of God was at hand, He invited us to Truth (with a capital "T"). "The truth," He declared, "will set you free" (John 8:32).

It's true.

This is why people confess their wrongs even when they don't have to. Beneath the churning pool of desire lies a yearning to be set free by truth. Like iron filings self-arranged around a magnet, the soul finds repose when it is aligned with truth—even uncomfortable truth. The truth lights up the whole world, revealing the road that we travel and clarifying its destination. The truth really does set us free.

The soul was made for truth. Truth is why we explore, investigate, create, calculate, and even imagine. Because, in spite of the war that desire has declared on truth, all of us know, somewhere in our souls, that truth will have the final say. Myth may drive us, but truth purifies us. Truth has wings.

My friend Daniel McCoy has faithfully and winsomely addressed the struggle between desire's myth and fact's truth in this book. He has pointed out that, though we may desire that certain things be just so, truth is far better. Desire whets the appetite, but truth feeds the soul.

Read this book and order your life around the truth. Listen as Daniel playfully deconstructs the deceits we wish to be true, and, in their place, gives us a truth that is infinitely better.

It takes courage to live by truth when the whole world prefers myth, but the strong person finds joy in truth's discovery and peace in its constitution. The real thing is just better.

"Teach me your way, O LORD, that I may walk in your truth" (Ps. 86:11).

It's true.

—Dr. David Young, senior minister of the North Boulevard Church of Christ, author of *A Grand Illusion: How Progressive Christianity Undermines Biblical Faith and King Jesus and the Beauty of Obedience-Based Discipleship*

# CHAPTER 1

## Two Kinds of Statements

The purpose of this book is to expose what doesn't exist so that we all can retrain our desires to focus on what does exist. We're about to start talking about turtles and death-defying trips to Mexico and all sorts of things. But let's keep the purpose of this book front and center: my heart is to help people by exposing the mirage, so that we can spend our time pursuing what actually exists.

---

One afternoon I was leaving the church where I worked, and I saw a turtle. I thought, *Nice little turtle.* I like turtles because they always seem fairly friendly, or at least never mean-spirited. Then I rounded the corner and saw two more turtles and had to change my view on turtles. I saw a big, bully turtle snapping at one-second intervals at a poor, little turtle which had its head tucked into its shell. I watched the littler turtle turn to make his getaway, with the bully turtle right behind him. Bully caught up to him and tried to climb onto his back. Meanwhile, the little one kept straining his neck out as far as it would go and making his face grimace. He looked as though he was crying for help, but no sound came.

The big turtle finally got off the smaller one. So I decided to go over and kick the big one. Not hard, but just enough to where he was going to pay attention to what I had to say: "You are being a bad turtle. You should look out for the little guy, not pick on him." Kick. "You're a big bully, and you should be ashamed." (It is possible that I was disturbing a moment of animal intimacy, but I prefer to think I was teaching a bully a lesson. Now that I think about it, if it was intimacy, it was probably totally fine. They were probably just married, having just come from the church and all.)

Satisfied that I had looked out for the little guy, I got in my van and put it in reverse. "Crunch." *Hmm. What was that?* And there, where my left back tire had just been, was the first (original) turtle with a (now) cracked shell. Out of the cracks bulged wormy organs and fresh sputters of ketchup. One leg quivered, waving a last goodbye to a cruel world.

Way to go, "Mr. Look-out-for-the-little-guy"!

---

This chapter is about two kinds of statements. The story I just told is meant to introduce the *second* kind of statement. But let's back up. Two kinds of statements . . . are they by chance *true* statements and *false* statements? Almost, but not quite. It has something to do with true and false, but it's a bit more complicated. Here goes. The first kind is:

*Statements that make themselves true.*

And the second is:

*Statements that make themselves false.*

First, let me explain the difference between a statement that simply *is* true and a statement that *makes itself* true. Bob is talking while his wife is on the phone. So his wife says into the phone, "Bob is talking. Hang on." That's a true statement, because it accurately reflects what is actually happening: Bob is talking. Let's say that she pauses her conversation and says to Bob, "Could we talk later? I'm on the phone." Let's also say that Bob reverts (as all of us do more than we'd like to admit) to toddlerhood, and he whines, "But I am talking!"

Pause.

Whereas "Bob is talking" is a true statement, "I am talking" goes beyond merely being a true statement. "I am talking" is a statement that *makes itself true*. By uttering the words "I am talking," he automatically makes the words come true. It's just like when Jack Black's Nacho Libre sings, "I am singing at the party." Those words he sang made themselves true.

Now, let's talk about the difference between a statement that simply *is* false and a statement that *makes itself* false. Forty-some years ago, my dad and a couple of his buddies decided to cross the border and spend an evening in Tijuana, Mexico. A drunk man stumbled their way and informed my dad that he owed him twenty-five cents for the song he had written for my dad. Now that was a false statement. What's more is the drunk was holding a beer bottle by its neck and looking at my dad with wild eyes; it wouldn't have taken much for him to bring the bottle up and crash it down onto my dad's head. What my dad said, however, went deeper than merely false. In the calm of complete courage, my dad said, "Uh—uh—oh—um—well—I—um—I—no—speak—*inglés*. I no speak *inglés*!" That statement was not only false, but—considering the English words that he used—the statement actually *made itself* false.

## Statements That Make Themselves True

The bulk of this book is about desires we have that fall under the second kind of statement. Thus, we'll be brief about the first kind: statements that make themselves true. Here are some examples: A person worries himself to death by saying repeatedly, "Something bad is going to happen to me." A person pesters a friend into anger by saying repeatedly, "You're mad at me." A person makes a child brave during a scary time by remarking, "What a brave boy you are!" A commercial makes you want a product by saying essentially, "You really, really want this!" Prosperity Gospel televangelists makes millions by preaching, "God wants His children to be wealthy!" I wake up to my three-year-old telling my five-year-old emphatically, "Yes, he *is* awake!" (They had been arguing in the living room about whether or not I was awake.) The statement makes itself happen.

## Statements That Make Themselves False

Again, there are lots of statements that are just plain false, but here we're talking about the kind of statement you don't have to check the encyclopedia to falsify. To prove it wrong, look no further than the statement itself. Check out these examples from movies: After the man says something clumsy, the woman calls him "illiterate." The man exclaims, "I am not illiterate! My parents were married!"[1] By trying to prove he's not illiterate, he's proving himself illiterate.

Or how about this example: Someone insinuates that another person is too literal to understand figures of speech. "Metaphors are going to go over his head." The guy responds, in all seriousness, "Nothing goes over my head. My reflexes are too fast. I will catch it."[2] Again, in trying to prove that he understands metaphors, he proves that he doesn't understand metaphors. It was an argument that made itself false.

And who can forget "Unikitty" from the *Lego Movie*[3]: "Here in Cloud Cuckoo Land, there are no rules! There's no government, no babysitters, no bedtimes, no frowny faces, no bushy mustaches, and no negativity of any kind." And when someone comments that Unikitty has "said the word *no*, like, a thousand times," Unikitty responds, "And there's also no consistency!"

Now for a couple tweets that make themselves false. The tweet begins, "Celebrity so-and-so says he'll move to this-or-that a country if such-and-such politician wins the Presidency. Share if you don't give a darn" (G-rated version). What's self-refuting about this tweet? Well, if you share it, then you are showing by definition that you, in fact, do give a darn. Here's another tweet, apparently taken from the Flat Earth Society: "We have members from all over the globe."

Speaking of social media, a local sheriff made headlines by posting an announcement that the county would temporarily be shutting down social media access. After all, the way people obsessed over and misused social media, it was clear that they needed to log off and take a break. In the sheriff's words:

> Due to the extensive and repeated misuse of Facebook and other social media applications within this jurisdiction we will be blocking all Allen County access to Facebook, Twitter, Snapchat, Instagram, Tumblr, and YouTube between February 28 and March 1.[4]

As you might imagine, social media users fought back with fire and fury. Within about twenty-four hours, there were 3,700 comments, such as, "Seriously I will lead a class action suit if this happens; this is infringing on my right to life and happiness and free speech!" Although they were designed to defend their need for social media, comments such as these merely confirmed what the sheriff had set out to prove: these poor addicts needed less social media in their lives. So obsessed with and dependent upon social media were they, in fact, that they hadn't even taken ten seconds to find out that there are no days between February 28 and March 1.

Do self-refuting *actions* count? If so, then let me tell you about my college job as a tutor in the "Learning Center." When we didn't have students to tutor or papers to proof, we would sometimes have competitions to see who could do more push-ups. It was one such uneventful afternoon, and it was just me and my boss, Shawn. I said, "Shawn, let's do a push-up competition."

"No."

"C'mon."

"Not today."

"You're a sissy."

Without a word, Shawn swaggered over to my desk with a pencil in his hand. *Boom!* He slammed the pencil down on the desk, not three inches from my face. He was holding the pencil between his fingers in such a way that you could break it with one good slam. And, sheesh, it was an intimidating, thunderous pounding. Except it didn't break. Again, without a word, Shawn slinked back to his office, his hand tremoring spasmodically, and shut the door behind him. A power move that made itself false.

Another self-refuting action happened while I was a tour guide for a college. My job was to conduct myself and my tour in such a way that I communicated how exciting and engaging the college was. This particular morning, I took my seat to the right of the prospective student at the biweekly chapel service. The sermon began. Fifteen minutes later, I woke up with my head tilted left so far that I was literally two inches from the prospective student's right ear. And why didn't I see him as a freshman in the autumn? Self-refuting action.

---

Here are some more quick examples of statements that make themselves false: I stumbled upon a want ad for a ghost-writer to take other people's articles, rewrite them, and "make them unique," and yet the ad said, "Any plagiarism we find will result in immediate termination of your contract."

Multiple times, I've seen an insurance packet that has a blank page all except for a small-print line in the middle: "This page is left intentionally blank."

I used to teach writing and I would assign an annual research paper. According to the textbook we used, page two of the research paper was to be the "pledge page." Basically, a pledge page is two paragraphs in which the student states that there is no plagiarism in the research paper. It's a pledge that nothing word-for-word was quoted without quotation marks. Nothing was taken from a source without putting the source in a footnote. The irony is that the students were supposed to copy the two paragraphs *directly* from the textbook—word-for-word, with no quotation marks, no footnotes.

One year as I taught tenth-grade language arts, one of the assignments was to use the new vocabulary words in original sentences. One of the new words was *veracity*. It's a noun, meaning "correctness, accuracy." Here's a sentence one of my students wrote: "If you don't know what a word means, look the word up so that you can be veracity." And I thought: *She probably should have looked up the word "veracity."*

Comedian Steve Martin has been known to respond to fans with letters reassuring them that, unlike other celebrities, he genuinely values their relationships. Here's an example of one such letter. The regular text is pre-typed, and only the blanks are handwritten (with what is in parentheses).

Dear ___ (*Jerry*),

What a pleasure it was to receive a letter from you. Although my schedule is very busy, I decided to take time out to write you a personal reply.

Too often performers lose contact with their audience and begin to take them for granted, but I don't think that will ever happen to me, will it ___ (*Jerry*)? I don't know when I'll be appearing close to you, but keep that extra bunk made up in case I get to ___ (*Flint*).

Sincerely,
___ (*Steve Martin*)
Steve Martin

P.S. I'll always cherish that afternoon we spent together in Rio, walking along the beach, looking at ____ (*rocks*).[5]

One student decided to write a paper in my class on how to make no-bake cookies. Not knowing the first thing about it (and probably the day before it was due), he asked his classmates, in all seriousness, "How long are you supposed to bake no-bake cookies?"

And then, of course, there are the statements my own kids have said that make themselves false or that collapse back in on themselves in some way.

"She's tattling!"

"Stop yelling!!"

"I'm not angry!!!"

At the table, I've heard multiple times, "She's not closing her eyes during the prayer." My eldest thought she'd learned a new word ("gibberish") and decided to use it on my wife: "Mommy, you're speaking gibbish."

Sometimes a person trying to explain something will get tongue-tied and will finally concede, "Well, it makes sense in my mind; I just can't verbalize it." This much can't even be said for the second kind of statement—statements which make themselves false. Such statements can't even make sense in the mind if thought out. Why? Because such statements are actually non-things.

"Can God make a stone so big that He can't lift it?" It's a fairly puzzling dilemma until you realize that if you're able to make the stone, it would be an impossibility not to be able to lift it. Such a scenario is a non-thing, akin to a married bachelor or a calculus course for preschoolers. The same could be said of God taking away the possibility of evil while at the same time giving us free will. It's a non-thing to have a scenario in which there is both the possibility of evil (free will) but no possibility of evil.

## Why This Book?

The reason for this book is that many people desire non-things. Rational, likable people spend their lives pursuing desires that make themselves impossible. I wrote this book because I want to spare them the disappointment that will come so long as they continue to desire what turns out to be a mirage. I want them to want what *exists*. So the purpose of this book is to expose what doesn't exist so that we can all retrain our desires and redirect our trust to what *does* exist and what *will* satisfy.

Jesus once asked a couple blind men, "What do you want me to do for you?" (Matt. 20:32). *Umm, maybe You could make my eyes work?!* Crazy question, right? Not so crazy when you understand that many people want some really crazy things—often not even that. People want some really crazy *non-things*.

# CHAPTER 2

## Mirage #1: I Want God to Love Me
## By Affirming My Decisions.

*"So Cain was very angry, and his face fell."*
*—Genesis 4:5b*

Among France's cultural contributions to the world (fries, etch-a-sketches, the guillotine) is the flower game "He loves me; he loves me not." An eighteenth-century French girl would pluck flower petals to the stem to determine whether a boy she liked had a crush on her. "Silly," you say. Not so silly, however, as the game the boy likely played. Based on how guys think, my guess is that the boy would play the variation, "She loves me; she loves me lots." After all, he told himself as he powdered his face to pale perfection, "I look *good*."

Does God love us, or does God not? Now, of course, *love* here needs to be defined as more than a romantic crush on humans (we're not talking about Zeus, after all). And we don't necessarily use petals. But figuring out whether God loves us can be every bit as rhythmic, as predictable. *Bless these nachos. He loves me. Curse this diarrhea! He loves me not.* Back and forth, until the stem.

Isn't it true that some people seem to have flowers in which every petal smiles up at them? "Fee-a-ling very blayessed." At the same time, other people have flowers in which every petal seems engraved with an "I hate your guts. –God."

Just ask Cain. One of Cain's chronic characteristics is his grumpiness. Why does he consistently act as if his already-itchy, woolly mammoth underpants are in a wad? God preferred his brother Abel's offering to Cain's inferior offering. So how does Cain respond? "Cain was very angry, and his face fell" (Gen. 4:5). The anger grows to such an extent that just three verses later, Cain takes his brother into a field and kills him. When God confronts him because of the murder, Cain acts dismissive and sullen: "Am I my brother's keeper?" (Gen. 4:9). Then when God comes up with an extraordinarily lenient punishment for Cain, Cain overreacts like a drama queen who just got grounded: "My punishment is greater than I can bear" (Gen. 4:13).

Seriously, why so angry? Cain's anger seems to have begun when Cain got his feelings hurt. He felt judged by God and began to see himself as the unfavored, unloved one. After all, God had questioned Cain's motives. God had asked him, "Why are you angry?" (Gen 4:6). Then God went on to warn Cain of the consequences of what he was about to do: "Sin is crouching at the door . . . you must rule over it" (Gen. 4:7). And after Cain had gone through with the murder, God had made Cain feel guilty for what he had done: "What have you done?" (Gen. 4:10).

Brandishing a stem, an extinguished candle, the "final straw" in his fist, Cain glares heavenward. *He loves me not.* The last petals have fallen. So has Cain's face. The three final petals in particular have torn away at an increasingly bare and bitter soul: Last was the petal that asked, "What have you done?" *Cain, what you have done is wrong.* Second to last was the petal that said, "Sin is crouching at the door . . . you must rule over it." *Cain, what you're about to do is wrong.* Third to last was the petal that said, "Why are you angry?" *Cain, your heart is wrong.* Wrong, wrong, wrong!

If Cain is feeling unfavored, it might make him feel better to know that favoritism isn't foreign to Genesis. Just ask the brothers of Joseph. They tell themselves in disgust, *Just look at that gaudy coat.* The multi-colored coat is out-dazzled only by the greasy grin of its wearer. Then the brothers look down at their own plain brown cloaks, sequined only in the back and only because they typically have to sleep on ground strewn with sheep droppings.

Eyes half-closed, or half-open, depending on how optimistic you can be at six in the morning, Reuben, Simeon, Levi, Judah, Zebulun, Issachar, Dan, Gad, Asher, and Naphtali stumble into the house to see what's for breakfast. Something smells good!

Dad and Mom and stepmom and concubine and concubine are all busy in the kitchen cooking what smells like biscuits and gravy. The boys take their seats at the table, licking lips, more awake now, eagerly glancing at the adults in the kitchen who still have their backs turned. It's Reuben, the oldest, who speaks first: "Wow, that sure smells good!"

Jacob, their father, speaks up. "Thanks, Levi."

"Actually, Dad, this is Reuben."

"Oh, I'm sorry, Reuben. Well, boys, while we're finishing up in the kitchen, why don't you guys go ahead and have your breakfast. Bowls are in the cabinet. Budget Toasty Corn Squares are in the cupboard."

After a while, down the stairs descends Joseph, smiling ear-to-ear, wearing that ridiculous multi-colored coat. As he enters, Dad, Mom, stepmom, and both concubines turn around. Jacob smiles, eyes sparkling: "Good morning, my dear son, my beloved Joseph. How are you this morning? We made your favorite breakfast. Careful, plate's a bit hot. You sit down, and I'll bring it over."

"Thank you, father," says Joseph, watching the plate of biscuits and gravy make its way under his nose. The brothers look from their spoiled brother to their soggy cereal and back. "Oh! Brothers! How would you like to hear about the dream I had last night? You all were in it!"

There it was, as noticeable as a multi-colored coat: favoritism. But is *favoritism* the problem that Cain had from God—that somehow God loved Abel, but not Cain? Cain asks himself as he glares heavenward, *What else can you call it when*

*God questions your motives, gives you a bunch of warnings, and then makes you feel guilty for what you've done?*

Good question. What do you call it when someone questions your motives, gives you warnings, and makes you feel guilty for what you've done?

---

I was writing sections of my doctoral dissertation. Meanwhile, my supervisor was putting the "diss" back in dissertation. "Way to go"? Perfect chapter"? "You're awesome"? No. Try, "That's a little crass and not necessarily true. It really does not belong in a dissertation." "That's a little bit of a vacuous statement." "Daniel, that's a generalization that one simply cannot make." "What? Please find another word or delete the sentence." And then the comment that still makes me cringe: "That statement is as vague as it is unnecessary."

It didn't feel much like love.

And yet, Proverbs 27:6 says, "Faithful are the wounds of a friend; profuse are the kisses of an enemy." Why was my professor so direct in his criticisms of my dissertation? Simple: he cared about how it turned out. Thus, once the dissertation was submitted, I knew that his email message wasn't fluff: "You did an amazing job on your work."

Why had my professor told me things along the way that stung a bit to hear? It's because he cared about the finished product. If he had told me only things which would have been *fun* to hear, then that means he would have been indifferent to the dissertation's outcome.

Here's the mirage we want that doesn't exist: We want God to love us by affirming all our decisions. If we're honest, there are times when we are like Cain: We want God to love us by never questioning our motives. By never giving us uncomfortable warnings. By never making us feel guilty for what we've done. But love cannot be indifferent to our outcome! It's impossible for love not to care about how we turn out. If God loves you, then, by definition, He *cannot* affirm what hurts you, and—by definition—He *cannot* be indifferent to how you turn out.

What is it called when God's flashlight invades your heart's caverns to diagnose your motives? What's it called when God warns you what paths lead where, and when He grieves when you ignore his advice as nonchalantly as you would silence a phone? Here's what that's called: it's called *concern*. And there can only be one reason God is so concerned with how you turn out. It's because He loves you.

---

You decide to take up gardening. So you go to the store, buy a few tomato plants, and plant them. Then, every day, you take the hose and water the tomato plants. A few weeks later, your neighbor, Mrs. Gardner, who happens to be an expert gardener, decides to check in and see how your tomato garden is coming. You show her to the backyard, delighted to show off your accomplishment. When she sees it, Mrs. Gardner gasps, "Oh my! Where are the tomato plants?"

"Oh, they're in there, all right," you smile. "They're hidden in there deep, but they're in there."

Mrs. Gardner isn't impressed. "Well, what are all these nasty weeds doing in here?"

"Oh, come now, Mrs. Gardner! It's a garden, isn't it? A garden is where you grow things, and I just happen to be growing lots of things in my garden. Why, I'll bet your garden doesn't have half of the kinds of plants I've got here!"

Mrs. Gardner replies, "But don't you understand? You've got to get rid of the weeds in your garden for your tomato plants to do well. If you just let everything grow here, you're never going to get ripe tomatoes!"

"Oh, you're just a cranky old woman, Mrs. Gardner! You're jealous of my great big, lovely garden just bursting with life! Now, if you'll excuse me, I need to get back to watering my garden."

A shower of affirmation is easy; love is not.

---

When God tells you to repent, it's actually one of the most loving gifts you could ever be given.

Oscar Wilde's *The Picture of Dorian Gray*[6] is about a young man who, magically, never gets older; instead his painted portrait gets older. Anything bad that he does, no one ever finds out about it because it's always the hidden portrait that shows it, never he himself. So Dorian is invincible; he lives as he wants with no apparent consequences.

Dorian falls in love with a beautiful young actress. She's poor, but Dorian's very wealthy, so he can provide. They make a charming match—she, the beautiful actress and he, the wealthy gentleman.

On her next performance, Dorian brings some of his high society friends to watch. And to his disappointment, she messes up her lines. She's wooden. It's like she's forgotten how to act. So Dorian is really embarrassed. After the show, he complains to her how humiliated he is. And she tries to explain. She wasn't trying to put on a poor performance; it's just that, before she met Dorian, she'd never really known actual love. Now that she knows love, she can't seem to put herself into her acting anymore. Which is okay, right? Because Dorian and she are in love, and he'll take care of her.

But Dorian is just cold, cruel. He tells her that yeah, he used to love her, but now he doesn't know what he was thinking. She produces no effect anymore. She doesn't excite him anymore. Quite frankly, he doesn't want to see her again. Here's how the book puts it:

> She put her hand upon his arm and looked into his
> eyes. He thrust her back. "Don't touch me!" he cried.
> A low moan broke from her, and she flung herself at his
> feet and lay there like a trampled flower.

He leaves. Next morning, he wakes up. And he just feels awful for what he's done. He had been so cruel to her. He wants so badly to see her as soon as possible and apologize. But then he hears the news. She'd committed suicide the night before.

It's here that we realize the truth: The word *repent* isn't the word to be afraid of. No, the word to be afraid of is the word *regret*. *Repent* gives me the chance to make things right before it's too late. *Repentance* is God's gift to protect me from regret.

So you want God to love you by affirming all your decisions? Don't. That kind of love isn't love. A love which only affirms everything doesn't exist, and you wouldn't like it for very long if it did. We tend to take God's rebukes as somehow attacking *us*. Nothing could be further from the truth. Rather, He's attacking that which attacks us. Sure, a tumor can intertwine itself into a body, but the tumor is not the body. Being able to make this distinction is a matter of life and death.

No less serious is the distinction the apostle Peter makes between the soul and the soul's enemy: "Beloved, I urge you as sojourners and exiles to abstain from the passions of the flesh, *which wage war against your soul*" (1 Pet. 2:11). Sin is the soul's tumor. To destroy sin is to save the soul.

If your love is the real thing, then you'll hate what seeks to destroy what you love. Says the apostle Paul: "Let love be genuine. Abhor what is evil; hold fast to what is good. Love one another with brotherly affection" (Rom. 12:9–10a).

As my daughter Beth said as a five-year-old, regarding one of Disney's *Frozen* characters, the Duke of Weselton: "I like him, but he's also bad, and I don't like his badness."

You will be as unsatisfied as Cain so long as you close yourself off to love by demanding what doesn't exist. Getting a thumbs up to *all* your decisions isn't called "love." It's called "indifference." Asking God to love you by affirming all your decisions is to ask God to grant you a mirage.

So what *does* exist? A God who actually loves you, that's what.

The anxiety of a loving home is that parents are always asking themselves how they can prepare their kids for a cruel world that won't care about them. The hope of a cruel world, however, is that beyond it is an ultimate reality Who loves us more than even our parents could. In fact, His concern shows us that He loves us far better than we love ourselves.

# CHAPTER 3

## Mirage #2: I Want God to Fix Everything Without Touching Anything.

*"But when Pharaoh saw that there was a respite, he hardened his heart and would not listen to them, as the Lord had said."*
*—Exodus 8:15*

I heard a story about two fellas walking through a field. They spot a three-foot-in-diameter hole in the ground. From the edge, both peer down into what looks like a well without water. It's just a hole that goes—*well, just how deep does that hole go?* One tosses in a stick. They wait but hear nothing. The other throws in a stone. Nothing. *Maybe it's so deep that only something large will make a sound.* So they wrestle a railroad tie over and dump it in the hole. Then things get really strange. For, out from some trees, a goat sprints past them and jumps headfirst into the hole. *What?!* Then up walks a farmer who asks, "Have either of you boys seen my billy goat? The rascal must have run off. Well, he couldn't have gotten far. I tied him to a railroad tie . . . ."[7]

It's ironic that he was tied there for the sake of security.

A dog latches onto a chew toy. The human's holding the other end, and the dog's teeth are so latched onto the toy that the toy whips the dog back and forth in the air. It's possible with good intentions to tie yourself to something that jerks you back and forth.

---

It was quite a contrast: the suspendered old-timer on the moped admiring the gritty biker's Harley Davidson. The light had turned red when both men found themselves side-by-side, and the biker smirked at the old geezer's amazement. "I'll bet that motorcycle can go fast," said the senior citizen from his moped, leaning over to get a clearer look.

The old man was quite far-sighted. His shaky head and hands were getting a bit close to the bike, and the biker was getting a bit annoyed. So when the light turned green, the biker floored it, leaving the grandpa in the dust. Soon the moped was a dot in the mirror. Except it was a growing dot. The moped was catching up. No . . . it was passing him! Within seconds, the moped was a dot again, but this time it had left the Harley behind! It was clear now that the old guy was just messing with the biker, as the moped again slowed and let the Harley catch up. As they switched places again, the moped fell behind. But sure enough, here it came again. Too close this time, however, and the two bikes collided.

Both men lying on the highway, the biker yelled out, "What's the matter with you?! You trying to get us killed?!"

"No . . . I'm just trying to get my suspenders unhooked from your handlebars."[8]

Sometimes it's possible to tie your heart to something that jerks you back and forth without mercy. Sometimes, however, it's possible to tie your heart to something through which *you* jerk other people around without mercy.

For example, I have a thing for ice cream. When my daughter Sarah was four, she was eating her strawberry and banana frozen yogurt. Yogurt is not even ice cream, but even it has the power to give me a heart freeze when it comes to my ability to love my children. Sarah stopped to talk to Mommy, and I reached over and grabbed her bowl and kept it under the table where she couldn't see it. The following dialogue ensued:

Sarah: My ice cream! Where could it be?
*She walks around looking for it.*
Sarah: Where's my ice cream?
Mommy: Well, I don't have it. Who else could have it?
*(We're the only three people in the room.)*
Sarah: Huh?
Mommy: Well, I don't have it. So who else could have it?
Sarah: Who has my ice cream?
Mommy: Now remember, I don't have it. Who's left? . . .
Do you think Daddy might have it?
Sarah: *(Brightens up)* Daddy, did you eat it?
Daddy: Eat what?

Sarah: My ice cream?
Daddy: What about your ice cream?
Sarah: Did you eat it?
Daddy: Did I eat what?
Sarah: My ice cream?
Daddy: I love ice cream! What about it?
Sarah: Did you eat my ice cream?
Daddy: No.
Mommy: Ask him if he knows where it is.
Sarah: Do you know where it is?
Daddy: Where what is?
Mommy: *(hinting at what Sarah should say)* Do you know where the *ice cream* is?
Sarah: Huh uh.

Finally, I just handed it to her. Again, it's possible to tie your heart to something through which you jerk other people around.

---

I need to talk about a pharaoh for a moment. Now please don't take what I'm about to say as anything against all pharaohs. The ones I've seen look pretty harmless, even if their non-blinking stares are a little intimidating and their striped headdresses are a little over the top. But I can say without fear of exaggeration that there was one pharaoh who was officially a *jerk*. Not only was he a jerk, but, as we will see, this particular pharaoh latched onto something so doggedly that there was a lot of merciless back-and-forth jerking because he was such a jerk. But the million-dollar question will be this: Was Pharaoh the jerker or the jerked?

"Let my people go." *Heh heh. I've never even heard of this guy or his "God." I'm most certainly not going to let him leave the country with my workforce.* But then the Nile gets turned to blood. Later comes the frogs. "Okay! Okay! Just get rid of the frogs!" But when the frogs leave, so does Pharaoh's reason for letting the Israelites go. New reasons: "Okay! Just get rid of the lice!" "Okay! Just get rid of the boils!" "Just get rid of the hail, and I promise this time!" "Just get rid of the locusts, and you can go!" In this way he jerked Moses back and forth. Clever. Until we see what the back-and-forth is doing to Pharaoh's country. Or what it's doing to Pharaoh himself! It'd be called insanity if he weren't able to execute on command. So is the jerk the jerker or the jerked?

It's as if Pharaoh was vacillating between pleading with God and then responding to His interventions with iciness. Warm tears and then cold shoulder. "Please" and then "No thank you." "Do something!" but then the moment God does, "Your services are no longer required."

I suppose when you look at the context, Pharaoh's insane back-and-forth actually made some sense. You see, before Moses came along, all was right with the world for Pharaoh. Ever since the plagues, Pharaoh was just trying to get back to the way things had been before Moses. When Pharaoh pleaded for the plagues to go away, he was just trying to get back to life as normal. And then when Pharaoh said, "Actually, never mind," it was for the same reason: the pursuit of normalcy. He wanted to get back to the good old days of being unbothered by a higher power. Ah, the good old days. But let's not forget that the "good old days" were back when, at Pharaoh's command, Hebrew baby boys were tossed into the Nile as casually as skipping stones into a pond. Let's not forget that it was Pharaoh who stained the Nile blood red first.

And then the story takes a scary turn. It goes like this: You and I can be a lot like Pharaoh. We too really, really want things to get back to normal. For example, we want God to take away terrorism, bombings, sexual assault, holocausts, head-on collisions, and theft. Sometimes He allows terrible things which disrupt good lives, and we wonder why. *Why can't things get back to normal?* Now, it's not wrong to want life to go well. It's totally normal to want life to get back to normal. But, like Pharaoh, there are times when we can want normalcy so bad that we end up treating God like He's the dog latched onto the chew toy. In our attempts to get life back to normal, we can try to jerk God back and forth with a "please" and "no thank you," similar to Pharaoh.

In fact, a rather extreme form of this is found among numerous atheists whose books I have read. In one breath, these atheists argue, "God should do more to take away the evil in the world." In the next breath, they contend that God is a tyrant for trying to intervene in everybody's lives. Hang on. Why exactly does God try to intervene in our lives? Could it be because He's trying to rescue us from the evil which we say we want Him to get rid of? There are atheists who say that evil is such a terrible problem that they believe a good God can't even exist. Yet, at the same time, they think God is a terrible God for trying to get rid of the evil in us.

---

I know a baby boomer who wanted a Facebook account. Her husband was warning of Armageddon if she did, using every slippery slope argument in the book. So their son said he could sign her up for a Facebook account that would be so secure and anonymous that no one would ever even know it was her account. She could check other people's posts, but no one would ever know it was her. The son said when he got through with it, even the CIA would not be able to know that she was on Facebook. Not even the CIA, he assured her. The husband said, "Okay. If you can make it so secure that even the CIA doesn't know that she's on Facebook. But don't blame me if the house burns down." So the son set up his mom on Facebook. Within two days her sister-in-law had seen the account and messaged her. "So you finally got a Facebook account!!"

Sometimes things aren't as secure as they first appear.

That goes for the whole problem-of-evil argument. The whole "God must not exist because there's so much evil in this world" might sound persuasive at first. But the truth is, the existence of evil makes pretty good sense when you look at the larger context. Evil choices aren't good, but they are a byproduct of something God gave us that *is good*: human freedom. In the same way, diseases and disasters and all the other natural causes of death aren't good, but they too are a byproduct of something God gave us that *is good*: a lifetime. Can you imagine how hellish life on this planet would be if we didn't have lifetimes? We could be as evil as our imaginations took us, without ever suffering the consequences of decay or death. We could live forever, invincibly, without ever feeling the need to get right with God. A lifetime is so good that a wise person would consider it a gift. Yes, death is an enemy (1 Cor. 15:26), but even still, it's merciful that we humans are given a lifetime. When we realize that evil and death are bad byproducts of really good things, then it helps open us up to the possibility that God knows what He's doing.

The truth is, God *is* doing quite a bit to combat our problem of evil. It's just that He's doing it in a way that keeps our freedom intact. Obviously, God could have made us mindless robots who do whatever He programs us to do. Or He could somehow intervene every time that something evil is about to happen—so that, as C.S. Lewis put it, "A wooden beam became soft as grass when it was used as a weapon, and the air refused to obey me if I attempted to set up in it the sound waves that carry lies or insults."[9] But if God takes away the possibility of evil—or even just the really bad cases of evil—

then that's taking away a huge amount of human freedom. And if we don't have the ability to choose how we're going to live, then what's the point of making humans in the first place? Why not just make more animals?

There are three ways that God could conceivably rescue us from evil. They are:

A (for All)—God could prevent all evil by force.
B (for Bad)—God could prevent the really bad cases of evil by force.
C (for Conscience)—God could intervene to stop evil by working on us from the inside.[10]

Whereas A- and B-level interventions water down what it means to be human, C-level interventions are the best scenario for anyone who cares that humans stay human. So let's imagine what C-level interventions might look like. No, actually, let's not imagine it, since we don't actually need to use our imaginations. C-level interventions are precisely what we see when we look at the Bible. We see them in the Ten Commandments. We see them in God's reap-what-you-sow punishments. We see them in God's grace. We see them in God's work on our conscience through realizations such as, "Oh yeah, I'm going to stand before God someday"—another way of saying that we all die. We experience God's offer to transform us from the inside through His promises of heaven and warnings of hell. The God of the Bible specializes in transforming people who open themselves up to His interventions. If you're looking for someone who cares about both a) rescuing us from evil and b) giving us freedom, you won't find a bigger champion of these two things than the God of the Bible.

So how are we sometimes like Pharaoh? Well, think of the many people who complain that God doesn't do enough to fix evil (thus they're asking for A-level or B-level interventions), and yet they are completely resistant to God's mere C-level interventions in their own lives!

Here's what we want that doesn't exist: We want God to fix the problem of evil while not intervening in our lives. We want God to restore everything in our lives without changing anything in our lifestyles. We want Him to emancipate without intervening.

It is simply not possible for God to create the square circle that is being asked of Him. It is a non-thing to ask God to fix the problem of evil and, at the same time, to resist His offers to intervene in our lives. As C.S. Lewis puts it, "You may attribute miracles to Him, but not nonsense."[11] Put another way, God does miracles, but not mirages.

So like Pharaoh, we find ourselves going back and forth, unsure of what exactly we want from God. Do we want Him to rescue us or leave us alone? Our inability to coherently articulate what we want is reminiscent of Bernard in Aldous Huxley's *Brave New World*. Bernard was impressed by his friends' bravery (they were illegally destroying medicine that was harming people), but quite unsure what his response ought to be:

> Hesitant on the fringes of the battle. "They're done for," said Bernard and, urged by a sudden impulse, ran forward to help them; then thought better of it and halted; then, ashamed, stepped forward again; then again thought better of it, and was standing in an agony of humiliated indecision—thinking that they might be killed if he didn't help them, and that he might be killed if he did—when . . . in ran the police. Bernard dashed to meet them. He waved his arms; and it was action, he was doing something. He shouted "Help!" several times, more and more loudly so as to give himself the illusion of helping. "Help! Help! HELP!" The policemen pushed him out of the way and got on with their work.[12]

Back-and-forth activity can feel like we're doing something, but we just end up in the same place we began.

It's like Captain James Hook (played by Dustin Hoffman in the movie *Hook*[13]) who was threatening suicide to his first mate, Smee. He told Smee, "No stopping me this time, Smee. This is it. Don't make a move, Smee. Not a step. My finger's on the trigger . . . . Don't you dare try to stop me this time, Smee. Try to stop me . . . . Get over here! Stop me! This is not a joke!" All of the plus twos and minus twos lead us right back where we started.

Yet "back to where we started" is kind of the idea all along, isn't it? Normalcy. We ask God "Please" to get us back to life as normal, and that's the same reason we tell God "No thank you" when He offers to fight evil by transforming us.

Pickett's Charge at Gettysburg in the American Civil War was a Confederate infantry attack across a three-quarter mile field. Although meant to break the Union lines, most of the infantry never even made it to the stone wall behind which the Union was entrenched, being under heavy cannon fire the entire time. The attack was by all accounts a miserable failure, and some 6,000 Confederate soldiers died.

During a reenactment in 1913, Confederate veterans charged across the three-quarter mile field. This time, however, Union soldiers, overcome with emotion, jumped the stone wall and rushed out to meet the oncoming Confederates to embrace them. Blue extended the hand to gray, as brothers.

We naturally desire life as normal. That is, until we see what our sin has cost. Pharaoh may have stained the Nile red, but we've created plenty of ugly stains of our own. When we see things as they are (i.e., ourselves as *we* really are), we are no longer content with mere reenactment. We begin to actually want the interventions we've long asked for. May we stop preventing God from doing what we've asked Him to do. May we stop wanting what doesn't exist and start welcoming the One who does.

# CHAPTER 4

## Mirage #3: I Want God to Save Everyone Automatically.

*"We implore you on behalf of Christ, be reconciled to God."*
*—2 Corinthians 5:20b*

My senior year of college, I went on a mission trip to . . . Hawaii. Yes, it was a legitimate mission trip. In fact, for those who assume that it was just a baptized vacation, here's the truth: I almost died on that trip. The word that best described the trip isn't "baptized"; rather, it's "almost drowned." The reason: I am a Kansan who has no place being on a surfboard.

The process of surfing, as I understand it, goes like this: You lie on your board, wait for a wave, see a wave, paddle like crazy, try to stand, and then before you stand you fall into the water. Then repeat. Apparently they call the process "surfing." After a couple hours of paddling, standing, and falling, I'm tired. And thirsty from all the salt I've digested. I've fallen into the water so many times that the older fish have moved their children to safer areas in the ocean.

*Mirage*

Feeling queasy, I tell my buddies that I'm going to head to shore. But instead of letting me paddle the surfboard the 400 or so feet back to the beach, one former buddy asks for the surfboard. He says I shouldn't be needing it, after all. So without my surfboard and without any energy, I start swimming and staggering back to the shore. For the most part, the water's just up to my chest, which means I'm less likely to drown. And it also means I'm more modest, which I have heard is hottest, at least in my case.

However, about 300 feet from the shore, I take a step, and suddenly the water's over my head. Okay then, I'll swim. Yet as I try to swim, a wave apparently passes over, carries me forward, and then back to where I started. Then repeat. It's almost as if my hundred or so falls into the water are like one too many forgotten password attempts, so that now I'm locked out and can't try anymore. The ocean has locked me out of moving forward. I can't move forward, and I can't find my footing. I try poking my head out of the water, only to have my mouth and lungs sloshed with more salt water.

Six or seven minutes later, I haven't moved, though not for lack of trying. *Okay. I seriously need help.* So next time my head emerges, I try to tread water long enough to motion over a passing surfer. Within moments, a red and white surfboard is speeding toward me. The lifeguard is tall, muscular, and tanned—everything I'm not. He has muscles in places I don't even have places.[14]

I climb on his surfboard, turn around and say, "Thank you so much." Then, I think, *Here, this guy just saved my life, and I don't have anything to give him in return.* Then in a flash the answer comes. *Bingo! I know what I can do!* I turn back around, facing frontward, and throw up on his surfboard.

Here's the main lesson I learned that day: Having to get saved isn't a cool thing.

---

It's true that in church we use the term "getting saved," and it makes sense. It's not necessarily confusing or uncool. But think about the concept of having to "get saved." It's kind of humiliating. Definitely not a cool thing to have to admit about yourself.

And, speaking of churchy terms, here's a related statement that is even less cool than "I got saved." It goes like this: "*You* need to get saved."

Why is telling someone, "You need to get saved" so pesky? Offensive even? Let's be honest: it would be different if conversion to Christianity were presented simply as one life-enriching option among other life-enriching options. Yet it's presented in the Bible as one option of only two. There's an uncomfortable urgency. The pressure's on. Nobody likes being told they are on the path to eternal destruction. And no kindhearted person enjoys telling that sort of news. Evangelism literally means telling the "good news," and I personally believe it is great news. But that doesn't mean it is fun to paint the backdrop of sin and judgment, which is the only backdrop against which the gospel can come across as good news.

There is a way to sidestep the pressure to do evangelism and still feel okay spiritually. It's by becoming a religious "pluralist." A religious pluralist is somebody who believes there are *many* religious paths to find salvation. So it doesn't matter whether you're a Christian, Buddhist, Muslim, Hindu, Wiccan, or whatever. The pluralist views the many religions as paths up the same mountain, helping everybody reach the same heavenly summit.

So if you become a pluralist, then, in your mind, you've just run most of the world through an automatic salvation wash. That feels great because, if we're honest, we like when things work automatically. Automatic soap dispensers for germaphobes. Automatic card shufflers for bridge players. Automatic weapons for deer hunting.

We equally have an impulse for the automatic when it comes to spiritual matters.[15]

---

I needed a ride to an out-of-town car dealership (in case I needed to drive back a new car), so Dad drove me to check out the vehicle. After seeing a $300 "documentation fee" on the printout, I asked if the salesman could itemize the fee for me. He left and returned with the dealership's finance manager. Big smile, slick hair, snappy clothes.

"I'm just going to be honest with you. This fee is just extra profit for us. But legally we've got to charge it, because we charge everyone else it." Sounded a little circular. Oh well. Turns out I wasn't interested in the vehicle anyway, and the extra $300 was a nail in the coffin.

Time to go. Except the finance manager wasn't done being honest. Their "documentation fee," he explained, was not unlike court fees that he often has to pay because of his heavy foot.

Then he started telling us his life story. He didn't end up going to college because he got his girlfriend pregnant in high school. He'd been through three marriages and was working on a fourth. He'd found that potential wives were a lot like used cars; you needed to figure out what mileage was left in them.

Well, Dad and I are pastors. And while I was trying to shut the conversation down by avoiding eye contact by pretending the wall décor was interesting (why can't some people read body language?), my Dad was starting to feel for the guy and began trying to view him through pastoral eyes.

"You know," said Dad gently, "my parents were divorced too. So I know how hard it can be. And I've helped a lot of people who've been through divorce. If you like, I'm a pastor—"

"Well, isn't that a coincidence!" interrupted the finance manager. "I'm a pastor too!"

Why help someone when they're *already where they need to be*? It's nice to witness such automatic spiritual advancement.

Automatic, universal salvation would be great, wouldn't it? It would feel great to interact with people of other religions minus any of the pressure of wondering about the person's eternal destiny. After all, Christian evangelism is an uphill and unpredictable process.

Except *automatic* doesn't always work, does it? When she was three, my daughter Sarah came to me looking hurt.

"What is it?" I asked.

She held out her finger and told me that it had a boo-boo.

"Sarah, you know what will make your finger feel better?"

"What?"

"A hug!"

So she climbed on my lap, and I gave her a big, long hug. And I noticed as I was hugging her, she was holding up her finger and watching it. I gave her the hug, I sat back, and Sarah frowned. Still looking at her finger, she said, "No better."

As nice as it would be, religious pluralism doesn't actually make things better. It just doesn't work. Here are four reasons pluralists give for why we should rush everybody through pluralism's automatic salvation wash. But, as you'll see, none of the four reasons are very convincing.

1. **They're all the same.** Why should we see all religions as paths up the same mountain? Well, the pluralist explains, all the religions, at their core, teach the same basic truths. Like, "Don't kill. Don't steal. Don't lie."

It is definitely true that you can find solid ethical teachings in all the major world religions. However, beyond ethics, "they're all the same" gets very little mileage. It's hard to find anything more different than Jesus is God (Christianity) versus Jesus is not God—and to say he is God is to blaspheme (Islam). Or salvation comes by grace through faith (Christianity) versus salvation is attained through right technique (Buddhism). Or there is one God in three Persons (Christianity) versus there are millions of gods (Hinduism). And, obviously, these are just a few of the most fundamental differences. Add in other religions, and you'll get more pieces of evidence than you can count that the religions differ from each other in major, core ways.

2. **Even if they're not all the same, they're all symbolic.** This second reason says that religious claims are, at best, symbolic and not to be taken as describing ultimate reality. Therefore, the religions are all basically our best guesses to get at something we can't actually understand. We are told, "We can't really *know* anything about God, after all."

"Oh really? Why not?" we might respond.

And here's a pretty typical response: "Oh, you know. We can't know anything about God since God is so infinite and transcendent and eternal that we could never know anything about Him."

"Okay, besides being 1) infinite, 2) transcendent, 3) eternal, 4) unknowable, and 5) presumably existing, is there anything else you know about this unknowable God?"

To say that our Scriptures can't tell us accurate information about ultimate reality is ridiculous. If God created us, then why on earth would He be unable to tell us truth about Himself? After all, He's already communicated quite a lot about Himself simply by creating us and our world.

3. **Even if they're not all symbolic, God is love.** This third reason why we should believe all religions to be equally valid is a bit cheap. We are told that, since God is love, then everybody in every religion will be saved.

However, love isn't God's only characteristic, and even if it were, love shouldn't be used as a vague principle to predict whatever a person wishes to be true.

Biblically, God's love is anything but vague; it's actually quite concrete. Just think about it this way: how do we *know* that God is love? Is it because we feel summer breezes, hear bird songs, and see sunrises? But then we also feel famines, hear tornado sirens, and see loved ones waste away from cancer. How do we *know* God is love? Is it because that's the universal teaching of the major religions? Hardly: one commissions the caste system,[16] another tries to seduce Gautama away from enlightenment,[17] and another "loveth not transgressors."[18] How do we know God is love? For such a widespread assumption, one would think its source would be obvious. And it is: we discover that God is love from the Cross.

But why think that the Cross is love? How do we know it's not just a tragedy? Well, because the Cross was Jesus willfully taking our place. *Why take our place?* He took our place because He was paying the penalty for sin (Isa. 53:5; Heb. 1:3).

In short, one cannot separate God's love from His wrath against sin. Yes, God is love, and we know He's love because it's set against the backdrop of His being painfully clear on what is evil and false. Far from proving pluralism, God's love motivates evangelism:

> All this is from God, who through Christ reconciled us to himself and gave us the ministry of reconciliation; that is, in Christ God was reconciling the world to himself, not counting their trespasses against them, and entrusting to us the message of reconciliation. Therefore, we are ambassadors for Christ, God making his appeal through us. We implore you on behalf of Christ, be reconciled to God (2 Cor. 5:18–20).

4. **Even if God isn't love, at least we are.** This fourth reason is the pluralist saying that, even if the God-is-love argument fails to prove pluralism, at least pluralists are loving, and if anyone is truly loving, he too will become a pluralist. However, this kind of "love" is love only if Gautama, Zoroaster, Muham-

mad, Mahavira, Nanak Dev, Krishna, Jesus, and others were *wrong* when they taught that eternity is what ultimately counts. For the pluralist "loves" people insofar as he wants people not to suffer anxiety about the afterlife, guilt over unforgiven sin, or disharmony over religious turf. But what if there is an ultimate reality beyond (which is what all religions do teach)? If there is an ultimate reality beyond this life, then wouldn't love concern itself with helping others get there?

So the pluralist runs each religion through the automatic salvation wash. Yet automatic salvation in the Christian sense (and arguably, in the sense of the other religions as well) isn't just hard to pull off. By definition, automatic salvation doesn't exist. It can't. It's a non-thing. It's a mirage.

For what *is* Christian salvation? It's not something that can simply be done to people as if they were under anesthesia. Christian salvation is an altogether more involved process that involves the whole being. In fact, if we were to ask God to play word association, we would say "salvation," to which God would reply "marriage." He uses words like "bride" for the Church and "husband" for Himself, and the relationship is described as fueled by the deepest of loves. This is why the prophets made clear that apostasy equals affair, just as idolatry equals adultery:

> You have played the whore with many lovers; and would you return to me? declares the LORD . . . . Return,

faithless Israel, declares the LORD. I will not look on you in anger, for I am merciful, declares the LORD; I will not be angry forever. Only acknowledge your guilt, that you rebelled against the LORD your God and scattered your favors among foreigners under every green tree, and that you have not obeyed my voice (Jer. 3:1b; 12b–13).

One can restore motorcycles, paintings, and houses without their say. Salvation is also a restoration, but of human souls to their original intention. And the soul happens to be the only thing on the planet that cannot be restored against its will. If a soul is restored against its will, then it hasn't really been restored, has it? Anyone who thinks that God should "just save everybody" is missing the point of salvation. Salvation against someone's will isn't *salvation* in a biblical sense.

Salvation by automation doesn't exist. Salvation by grace through faith does.

# CHAPTER 5

## Mirage #4: I Want to Find Peace Through Trusting What I Can't Trust.

*"And Elijah came near to all the people and said, 'How long will you go limping between two different opinions? If the LORD is God, follow him; but if Baal, then follow him.' And the people did not answer him a word."*
*—1 Kings 18:21*

When I was in junior high, I was told to write a descriptive essay with lots of colorful descriptions. I giggled wickedly as I planned the story. It would read like a happy children's story but end with a dark twist. I decided to write about Tommy and Billy jumping in their pile of autumn leaves.

> "Yay!" "Hooray!" Lucky, not wanting to be left out of the reverie, bounded through the doggy door and into the fun, not noticing the snake that had slithered into the pile. "Bark!" Lucky yelped. Dad ran out, bent down to the dog, and said, "I'm sorry, boys. The dog is dead." The end.

*Mirage*

What is the thing we want? We want something in life that doesn't end like my pathetic story. Just one thing. Yet we get scammed by life at every turn. You amass stuff? Stuff rots. You pursue pleasure? Happiness eludes. You seek health and beauty? Food for worms. You trust leaders? Leaders disappoint. You love people? People die. Can you construct one of the great civilizations? They all crumble. Can you construct one of the great philosophical systems? They get entombed in history by philosophy textbooks soon after the death of their founders. Everything ends with the dog dead.

We want something we can trust. But that's only half the story.

---

In high school, there was a rather strange girl I had seen but never talked to. Yet I kept hearing people say that she had a crush on me. Moreover, they told me how the crush began. She had seen me around, but that wasn't why. Rather, she had seen a t-shirt of the band I was in, with our black-and-white, grainy picture on the back. From the picture, she determined that, contrary to what she'd already seen, I was actually good-looking. Again, the photo was pretty grainy. Moreover, I was wearing an oversized suit jacket that made me look way more muscular than I really was. Weird reason to have a crush, isn't it? The real me had nothing to do with it.

Take all the things humans obsess over. Newer vehicles. Political victories. Celebrity status. Forbidden pleasures. Boundless intellect. Flawless beauty. Fortified finances. Indestructible relationships. Humans obsess over *images* of these rather than over the real things. Humans read into their obsessions an ultimate dependability that not one of these things has ever actually demonstrated. Only in the imagination do such obsessions live up to such hopes. And even the mind tends to sober up after getting enough of the actual thing itself, so that it's time to move onto a new obsession.

In truth, do most people truly trust the religions in which they officially invest all their hopes? Think about it: I master the Noble Eightfold Path and achieve nirvana. I submit to Allah and achieve paradise. I foment revolution and achieve the classless society. I develop humanity and achieve humanism's heaven on earth. I assert my truth and achieve existentialism's authenticity. In other words, I may be claiming that I'm putting my faith in this or that object, but I really end up putting most of my trust in something I mostly can't trust, namely in *myself.* All along, our religions—both priest-centered and individualized—end up making us place trust in ourselves, whom we cannot in good conscience trust. Is it any wonder that we have trouble finding authentic peace?

———————————————————————————

We meet a king in the Bible who tried to put his trust in something that he didn't actually trust. His is a rather pathetic story with a tragic ending. You want to hear it? Great! First, let's look at the backstory.

*Mirage*

The family through whom God chose to bring the world's Savior was the Jews. After the Lord rescued them out of slavery in Egypt, He led them to the land He promised them. The first three kings (Saul, David, and Solomon) ruled all twelve tribes in the land. However, Solomon's son showed himself to be a hard, wooden ruler rather than the bending, plastic-type. Because of this, the northern tribes split off and formed their own nation. In breaking off from the South, the northern tribes largely broke with the God of Abraham, Isaac, and Jacob as well. One northern king in particular led his nation definitively toward worship of a god of the neighboring Canaanites. The god's name was Baal, and the king's name was Ahab.

Ahab built Baal his own temple. He built Baal his own altar in the temple. He constructed poles for the worship of Asherah, Baal's consort (or mother). He commissioned hundreds of Baal's prophets for his palace. He hunted those of God's prophets that remained. Persecution, however, didn't stop God from periodically sending His prophets popping out into the open like prairie dogs to deliver Ahab a message.

A prophet named Elijah challenged Ahab to a contest to see which deity could "answer by fire." The same prophet popped up right after Ahab's administration murdered a man to steal his vineyard. Another prophet rebuked Ahab for going too easy on a captured king. A prophet named Micaiah predicted Ahab's defeat in an upcoming battle. These naysayers help explain why someone who should have been the happiest man in all the kingdom was often grumpy ("vexed and sullen," "went about dejectedly," "lay down on his bed and turned away his face and would eat no food"[19]).

Here's what is fascinating about Ahab: Most power-hungry people today would salivate at what Ahab had. He had the power to do whatever he wanted, *plus* a customized civil religion with hundreds of adoring prophets who told him whatever he wanted to hear. These prophets gushed Ahab's praise and rushed to assure him that whatever he wanted was precisely what heaven also wanted. Yet Ahab was consistently grumpy.

Nowhere is this irony seen more clearly than in the episode with the prophet Micaiah. There were 400 prophets of Baal who were predicting Ahab's success in a coming battle with Syria. For this particular battle, the king of the North (Ahab) had formed an alliance with the king of the South (Jehoshaphat). When King Jehoshaphat noticed that all the prophets were just saying whatever Ahab wanted to hear, he became suspicious. Isn't there a prophet of *God* that we could hear from?

"There is," Ahab admitted. "But I hate him, for he never prophesies good concerning me, but evil" (1 Kings 22:8). When the other king insisted on hearing from this prophet of God, Ahab caved and summoned him. Meanwhile, all the other prophets were predicting that the battle would be an astounding success. One prophet took a pair of iron horns and said, "Thus says the Lord, 'With these you shall push the Syrians until they are destroyed" (1 Kings 22:11). The rest of the prophets echoed their agreements: "Go up and triumph!" (1 Kings 22:12).

When the prophet Micaiah entered the room, everyone knew what to expect. Micaiah would be the one cloud in a blue sky, the one curmudgeon against 400 optimists. They all knew what Micaiah would do: he would warn the king not to go to battle. Then the rest of the room would mock him and shout him down.

No one could have predicted what Micaiah would *actually* say. "Go up and triumph," Micaiah said to a shocked room. "The LORD will give it into the hand of the king" (1 Kings 22:15).

What?! Ahab couldn't believe his ears. This *couldn't* be the word of the Lord!

So Ahab thundered back in insane irony, "How many times shall I make you swear that you speak to me nothing but the truth in the name of the LORD?" (1 Kings 22:16).

Ahab already knew the truth.

And Micaiah knew the truth too. Micaiah went on to give the *true* oracle: "I saw all Israel scattered on the mountains, as sheep that have no shepherd" (1 Kings 22:17). All those voices predicting optimism were wrong. True to his character, Ahab would go on to rebel against Micaiah's true prophecy. He went into battle, was killed, and that day, true to the prophesy, Israel went on to become "sheep that have no shepherd."

What is fascinating about Ahab is that he knew the truth when he heard it. He ran from it. He recoiled from it as if it were nails on a chalkboard. All the same, he knew it was true. "How many times shall I make you swear that you speak to me nothing but the *truth*?"

What this suggests is that Ahab was never a true *worshiper* of Baal. The relationship was more like a contract. Ahab built Baal a temple and hired Baal prophets. In return, Baal did things like sent rain, gave aid in battle, and kept Ahab secure as king.

But truly *worshiping* what you know is inadequate? Wholehearted surrender? Complete trust? Ahab had to know that Baal was inadequate. After all, there was that time when Baal was unable to "answer by fire," whereas God was able to (1 Kings 18:29). And think about all the evil that Baal apparently was totally okay with. For example, Baal was completely fine with Ahab killing a man so that Ahab could make his land into an extra vegetable garden (1 Kings 21:15). Even if that's the kind of permissive god you like having around, it's not something you can put your wholehearted trust in.

So long as Ahab "worshiped" something he couldn't fully trust, he would never find peace. Ahab's heart would never find rest as long as he half-served what he half-trusted. Such a contractual arrangement is like lovers who only *use* each other. They go back and forth between thrill and resentment. But they never find lasting contentment. In the same way, Ahab used Baal's services, but would never find himself resting content.

What do we know about Baal? Baal was an Ancient Near Eastern warrior god with a helmet of horns. The "rider of the clouds" held in one hand a club and in the other a spear, signifying thunder and lightning respectively. As the storm god, Baal brought rain and fertility. Baal had conquered Yam, the god of the sea, only to be slain by Mot, the god of the underworld. On his way to the underworld, Baal had one last hurrah by mating with a heifer. However, it was not to be the end of Baal after all, for after his sister Anat killed Mot, both Mot and Baal were revived. The struggle between death and fertility continued, symbolizing the annual vegetative cycle.

We have one record of a prayer to Baal. Notice its contractual feel:

> O Baal! If you will drive the strong one from our gates, the warrior from our walls, a bull, O Baal, we shall dedicate, a vow, Baal, we shall fulfil, a male animal, Baal, we shall dedicate, a propitiation we shall fulfil, a feast, Baal, we shall prepare.[20]

Of course, this prayer is not from the Bible. When the Bible talks about Baal, it is typically in the genre of "smack talk" (1 Kings 18:26–29). For some reason, God was continually having to coax His people back from their affairs with Baal and other false gods, having to convince them that He was better for them. It should have been obvious to them that Baal was inferior to God in holiness and power. After all the greatness God had shown to His people, why wasn't His superiority obvious to His people?

Actually, it was.

In fact, it was God's superiority that was the *problem*. It seems that the people of God kept wanting something *less* imposing. *Less* demanding. *Less* holy.

---

If we're honest, we get tempted by modern-day Baals. Contracts with Baal survive in greed. In lust. In pride. Such contracts survive even in the church, where Sunday reveals one's religion, but who cares? Monday reveals one's god. Baal survives anywhere it can be said, "For my people have committed two evils: they have forsaken me, the fountain of living waters, and hewed out cisterns for themselves, broken cisterns that can hold no water" (Jer. 2:13).

The truth is, however popular (and tempting) deities such as Baal were in the ancient world, gods tend to go the way of Tommy and Billy's dead dog. Atheist H.L. Mencken pens a "memorial service" for dead gods, and goes on to list, with some glee, no fewer than 138 gods, of which he writes, "In the end they all withered and died, and today there is none so poor to do them reverence." Mencken is right. After all, science puts gods out of a job. Thor's hammer has a place in comic books, but not in science textbooks. For thunder and all manner of natural phenomena, we have scientific explanations. But does science put *God* out of job?

Despite Mencken's list, exasperated atheists watch religion continue to grow globally. How? Primarily through *monotheism*—specifically through the monotheistic religions of Christianity and Islam.[21] As Jeremiah predicts, "The gods who did not make the heavens and the earth shall perish from the earth and from under the heavens" (Jer. 10:11). Mencken might as well have been writing this prophecy's fulfillment. Science says to gods, "You're fired," but what does science say to the God who created an orderly universe in the first place? "Thanks for hiring me." Sure, the atheist would jump to add the God who "created the heavens and the earth" to the list of deities science has fired, but then the atheist is left having to explain how a "cosmic sneeze" is supposed to have set up the orderly and mathematically elegant lawfulness that allows science to work in the first place.

The truth is, even if God is proved bigger and better than whatever gods He is put beside, that doesn't stop us from feeling a mix of pity and longing for the lesser gods.

It's too bad that God is too big. God's bigness is why we settle for idolatry, the act of putting our trust in whatever allows us to keep our trust in ourselves (whom we know we can't trust). Couldn't God make Himself more like Baal in some ways? Less insistent on holiness, perhaps? Sorry: "For God cannot be tempted with evil, and he himself tempts no one" (James 1:13). How about less insistent on truthfulness? Again, no: "It is impossible for God to lie" (Heb. 6:18).

Our problems with God are not that He lacks in some area, but rather that He's simply *too* righteous (e.g., He can't overlook sin while remaining holy) and *too* rational (e.g., He can't take away suffering while giving us free will). And no one wants to room with an all-perfect Almighty God, let alone have such an imposing Presence room in one's heart.

However, there is a way God can grow smaller without growing less Godlike. How small are we talking? How about this: God as embryo. Seriously? Apparently, God felt it was worth a try. God spoke and it was . . . Christmas! The Son of God entered our world as an embryo.

However, there was another problem. For even as the idea of Baby Jesus, God Incarnate, made God more approachable, it also risked making God all the more susceptible to smack-talk. The earliest art depiction of Jesus is a crude graffiti image of a crucified man with a donkey's head, beneath which a man is kneeling. The caption: "Alexamenos worships his God."

It may seem stranger than anything to worship a crucified God, yet it is at the foot of the cross that we finally find something worth *fully trusting*: a God big enough to get small enough to save us from ourselves. He responded to our empty-headed transaction (trading God for gods) with an equally puzzling transaction of His own (trading Himself for us). And somehow through it all, He grew even bigger.

*So the choice is between big and small?* Not quite. It's more between something big that exists and something that doesn't even exist in the first place. We can try with all sorts of different gods, but at the end of the day, we can't fully put our trust in what we know we can't really trust. The result of seeking this mirage is a lot of irritation and no real peace. As the once aimless Augustine concluded, "You stir man to take pleasure in praising you, because you have made us for yourself, and our heart is restless until it rests in you."[22]

# CHAPTER 6

## Mirage #5: I Want to Find Freedom Through Sin.

*"Like a dog that returns to his vomit is a fool who repeats his folly."*
*—Proverbs 26:11*

My wife grew up in Iowa. Iowa is one of those places where most guys regularly hunt and fish; it's an epicenter of outdoorsiness. One New Year's Day while my wife and I were still just dating, I got to go up to Iowa and meet the entire family. We're talking grandpa, grandma, five uncles, five aunts, thirty-some cousins—all in one house for New Year's Day.

I get put in the living room with grandpa, uncles, and male cousins. Since it's New Year's Day, I ask the youngest boy cousin what he got for Christmas.

"I got a gift card."

"Where to?"

"Cabela's!" he says and smiles.

"Awesome!" I say.

"Yeah," he says.

"So, what is this *Cabela's*?"

Then the cousin practically yells, "You don't know what Cabela's is?!"

The living room falls dead quiet. Grandpa, uncles, and cousins all stop talking and look at me.

*Who invited this guy?*

A few years later, one of my brothers-in-law was invited to spend a summer in Thailand as an intern at a prison ministry. An intern's job isn't to give advice or teach; it's primarily to learn. And obviously, even if he were asked questions, he couldn't give much help when he didn't even speak the language. But there came a day when the guy in charge decided to ask his intern a question, because it had to do with the English language. *Oh, good! Finally, I'm being asked my opinion about something*, my brother-in-law must have thought.

"So, Intern, how do you spell the word *plane* in English? You know, like the plane you fly around in?"

And my brother-in-law said, "Oh. Yeah. Like you fly in. That would be—um—P-L-A-I-N. Plain."

(Spelling was never his thing. I'm reminded of the sticker I've seen that says, "Sure I was homeschooled, but that's neither hear nor their."[23])

Just then, a Thai person who was in the room spoke up and said, "Excuse me, but actually I think it is P-L-A-N-E."

And they all, of course, looked at my brother-in-law and thought, *Who invited this guy?*

It's like having a guy on your high school basketball team who tells grammar jokes while everybody is quoting funny lines from movies and talking about girls. On the basketball bench, he says, "Hey guys! Knock, knock."

*Silence.*

"C'mon, guys! Knock, knock."

*Collective scowl and eye-roll.*

"Knock, KNOCK!"

"Okay! Okay! Who's there?"

"To," he says.

"To who?"

"No . . . it's *to whom*."

*Who invited this guy?*

---

"Congratulations, you two!"

"Such a lovely wedding!"

"I just can't imagine a cuter couple!"

"Thank you, thank you!" the groom replies, grinning at his new wife and squeezing her hand.

Dignitary after dignitary, finely dressed, all smiles, warm congratulations. Until one particularly unkempt, crazy-haired, bulgy-eyed, camel-hair cloaked man appears, wagging his finger at the newly married couple. "It is not lawful for you to have your brother's wife!" (Mark 6:18).

Who invited this guy?

Actually, he wasn't invited. He was *sent*. In the Bible, God periodically sent prophets to kings in order to keep kings from getting a big head (even if this particular story will end with the king keeping a big head while taking the prophet's head too). The prophet is John the Baptist, and the monarch is Herod Antipas, with his new wife Herodias.

Herod Antipas, tetrarch of Galilee from 4 B.C. to A.D. 39, had been married to the daughter of an Arabian king named Aretas IV. Around A.D. 29, Herod lodged at the house of his half-brother Philip, where he fell in love with Philip's wife Herodias. To make matters even more like a soap-opera, Herodias was not only Herod's half-brother's wife, but also Herod's niece, the daughter of another half-brother. Herodias consented to marry Herod if he divorced his current wife, which he did. And they lived happily ever after—until John the Baptist said, "It is not lawful for you to have your brother's wife."

And no one took it harder than the blushing bride.

From that day on, Herodias looked for a way to kill John the Baptist. Why? Well, because, in Herodias's view, two adults are free to do whatever they want in the privacy of their own bedroom. And to say that the *king* of all people is doing what is "unlawful"?! So Herodias hated John the Baptist and actually felt justified in hating him. After all, wasn't John the Baptist hating her? Herodias saw it as hatred to try to disempower her with ancient prohibitions that were meant to enslave her. She was free to do what she pleased.

And it is true that John the Baptist was filled with hatred. He hated it when a married man shattered his wife's trust like it's an empty beer bottle. He hated it when a man stole another man's wife like marriage is a dance. He hated it when the highest ruler exemplified the lowest ethics.

He hated *it*.

But John the Baptist did not hate *her*. When he rebuked Herod and Herodias, it was spoken with aching sincerity. Knowing John, he was concerned with their soul. What's more is that John's passion for God's moral law wasn't overblown passion. We have all seen enough self-absorbed sexuality hurt enough people that we shouldn't disagree with John at all.

Still, Herodias was angry enough that she pressured Herod to lock John away. So there he was, beneath their feet in the downstairs dungeon. Everyone upstairs drank and laughed and partied. Herodias had her new husband in her arms. She had John in chains, silenced and neutralized. She had everything she wanted. And still, she seethed.

---

*The Stupids*,[24] made in 1996 and starring Tom Arnold, remains one of the unsung classics of cinematic history. When the Stupids (last name of the family) discover that their trash has been stolen *again* (it keeps happening week after week when they keep accidentally leaving their garbage cans out on the curb), this simple suburban family (with an emphasis on the word *simple*) decides to take matters into their own hands. On his rollerblades (after all, eight wheels is better than a car's four), Stanley Stupid (the dad) follows the garbage truck all the way to what he concludes must be the crime of the century ("There must be thousands of people's garbage here!"). Turns out the evil lair is a real dump.

Long story short: in the process, the Stupids actually and unknowingly end up stumbling upon a gang of illegal weapons dealers, whom they still believe are merely stealing garbage. During the final confrontation in a warehouse, a portion of the warehouse catches on fire. Ever the safety-conscious mother, Joan Stupid goes in search of a fire extinguisher. She finds one, but it is rather small, and next to it is a larger one. As soon as she grabs the larger extinguisher, however, she sees still a larger extinguisher. At last, she decides simply (there's that word again) to grab an even larger one: the largest one she's ever seen. She pulls the lever, and out shoots a huge flame. It's a flame thrower. After a few seconds, she releases the lever and says, "This is the worst fire extinguisher I've ever seen!"

Here is wisdom: Whatever Herodias is doing to extinguish the fire raging within her isn't working. Even putting the prophet in prison did nothing to alleviate her anger.

A few years ago, in our kitchen, the potholder on the oven caught fire. All I knew, however, was that the smoke alarm was going off. So like an idiot, while flames danced menacingly atop our stove, I went over to the smoke alarm and started mechanically waving a towel under it, while my wife actually put the fire out. It's not enough to fight the symptoms (e.g., "I'm angry at being told I'm wrong!"). We have to consider the source (e.g., "Maybe what I did was actually wrong.").

We all crave freedom. Freedom to do what we want to do and be what we want to be. Freedom to move about. Freedom in the relationship. In fact, freedom is how both political parties get their votes: by promising freedom and by warning of the freedoms lost if the other party gets in power. In a post-Christian culture, freedom edges toward the front as being one of our most sacred values. Not surprisingly, since we in the West pride ourselves as being the freest people on the planet, any threats to our freedom are met with 1776-era rifle-like resolve.

Credit cards set us free, right? Take it to the mall—new clothes. Take it to Home Depot—new drill. Take it to Best Buy—new 70" flat screen TV. Take it to Ashley Furniture— new dining room set. Amazon—click, click, click, two-day shipping. Credit cards set us free to buy whatever we want, whenever we want it.

Question: Are credit card addicts really *free*? Free to use it, yes. But . . . truly *free*?

*Mirage*

I may be reminded by monthly statements—then phone calls—that my debt is mounting. Yet by then, I have come to *need* that new gadget or garment. Perhaps I can't afford it, but that's not the problem I'm obsessing over. The problem is that I've got to have it. So I continue to swipe, swipe, swipe. Because I'm free to use it. But am I free *while* I'm using it? That's a different question.

Maybe you've got a shopping addiction. Drug addiction. Porn addiction. Eating addiction. Explosive anger addiction. Cussing addiction. Gossip addiction. Free to do all of the above, yes. But, all the same, not so free, are you?

We never seem to be as free as we want to be. Do you know what we really want? We want to be as free as the Herods. If there's a group of people in the Bible who are most free to do whatever they want—whatever their imagination tells them might be fun—it's the Herods. So Herod goes ahead and divorces his wife and marries his niece, who is also his brother's wife. *Why not?* Herodias moves in, and brings her daughter with her, a girl named Salome.

Think chess: In this story, you've got a king, a queen, and a pawn. First, the king. Now, can you imagine anybody telling the king—telling the "Law"—that what he is doing is *unlawful*? And all because of something as personal as sexual sin! Sounds especially foreign in our culture, where most people's response is to ask, "You mean there's such a thing as sexual *sin?*" People figure that whatever you want to do with whomever you want to do it is totally fine. If it feels good, just do it.

But John the Baptist says differently. He looks at the king and says, "That's sexual sin." The king says, "What are you talking about? I make the laws around here." John the Baptist says, "Nope, what you're doing is *unlawful*," which of course implies that there must be a Law higher than our laws.

Enter the queen. John the Baptist upsets the wife way more than he upsets Herod himself. In return, day and night, Herodias fantasizes about how she can get John the Baptist killed. Her chance comes when her daughter makes her entrance:

> But an opportunity came when Herod on his birthday
> gave a banquet for his nobles and military commanders
> and the leading men of Galilee. For when Herodias's
> daughter came in and danced, she pleased Herod and
> his guests. And the king said to the girl, "Ask me for
> whatever you wish, and I will give it to you" (Mark
> 6:21–22).

"Hooray!" says Herod. "I get to see my half-brother's ex-wife's daughter and the daughter of a different half-brother's daughter dance!" And it isn't your wholesome do-si-do barn dance. Suffice it to say that the dance is so provocative that Herod is overwhelmingly pleased. So pleased that he offers the girl whatever she wants.

*Mirage*

Salome's probably twelve to fourteen years old. What would a girl her age want from the king? Strangely, she doesn't answer. Instead, she walks out. Her mother is waiting.

And she went out and said to her mother, "For what should I ask?" And she said, "The head of John the Baptist." And she came in immediately with haste to the king and asked, saying, "I want you to give me at once the head of John the Baptist on a platter." And the king was exceedingly sorry, but because of his oaths and his guests he did not want to break his word to her. And immediately the king sent an executioner with orders to bring John's head. He went and beheaded him in the prison and brought his head on a platter and gave it to the girl, and the girl gave it to her mother (Mark 6:24–28).

Okay. Now, in the chess game, who's the king? *Herod.* Who's the queen? *Herodias.* Who's the pawn? Whose dance so delighted Herod? Whose request so relieved Herodias? That would be *Salome.* Salome's the pawn. She's the enablement of both parents' obsessions. Poor thing. Just look at her—throwing herself before a lusting group of drunks. She's an object of pity even though, yes, she was the one who ordered the platter. She's merely a pawn.

Those Herods, I tell you! Typically, you don't steal your brother's wife (maybe somebody else's wife, but not your brother's wife)—the Herods do. Typically, you don't marry your niece—the Herods do. Typically, you don't chuckle while your drunken friends lust after your step-daughter—the Herods do. The Herods do whatever they want. So . . . the Herods are completely free, right?

Your friends who are sleeping around: Completely free, right? Classmates getting high and needing the next fix: Completely free, right? Your friends looking at porn or sending each other porn: Completely free, right?

So who was the pawn again? Salome. And yet: Is the king really free? Not married to a woman like that, he's not! And just look at the guy's untamable lusts. He's a slave to his lust. Is the queen really free? The lady can't even see straight, she's so angry. She's so angry she gets excited about seeing the head of a prophet on a platter. I don't know what you call that, but it sure isn't free.

There's a king, a queen, and a pawn? Nope. There's a pawn, a pawn, and a pawn.

Jesus answered them, "Truly, truly, I say to you, everyone who practices sin is a slave to sin" (John 8:34).

---

"A slave to sin." True freedom isn't doing whatever you feel like doing. No, doing whatever you feel like doing all the time is how you become a slave. Learning to say no to what is shameful is not giving up your freedom; rather that's called keeping your freedom. Telling yourself *no* is how you stay out of slavery.

You cannot find liberation in an enslaving capitulation. You may want freedom through sin, but it's a mirage. Freedom through sin is a non-thing, and as such, it will disappoint every time you try it.

---

I got sick a few years ago on Christmas Eve. As I've done with numerous moving events in my life, I wrote a song about it. And it has everything to do with true freedom. This song is meant to be sung to the tune of "Rudolph the Red-Nosed Reindeer." It's called "Daniel the White-Faced Monster."

> While the tree lights are gleaming and children are dreaming
> Something is funny down deep in my plumbing
> Allow me to recall the most moving Christmas Eve of all
>
> I feel rumbling but not from the roof
> Pitter patter from inside
> Strange sounds but not reindeer hoofs
> My tummy's going for a ride
>
> Something is coming real fast
> But I don't think it's Santa Claus

Instead I think I'm discovering
An exception to gravity's laws

So that groggy Christmas Eve
My food came back to say
You wondered if your food was cooked
You can have a closer look

Then all my dinner came back
As it shouted out, "We're free"
Run away from the white-faced monster
Jump into the swirling sea

Matching the shade of color
Of the toilet by which he lay
Filling up stuff like Santa
Chunky in a different way

And as the last remnant left my stomach, I felt *free*.
Free from the junk that had awakened me at midnight first
hoping that it was nothing, then finally—once the discom-
fort passed a particular threshold—just hoping to get it
over as soon as possible. That, I suppose, is the same way
with enslaving habits: you hope it's nothing until it gets
bad enough that you're finally ready to be free of it. That, I
repeat, is freedom.

This, I must stress, is freedom's opposite: "Like a dog that returns to his vomit is a fool who repeats his folly" (Prov. 26:11).

The fool feels free. But the glutton becomes a slave to his gut. The fool finds himself chained by his own unrestraint. The proverbial wild duck who feeds on barnyard food for an hour, then a week, then the summer, and so on finds himself too heavy to join the duck formation when they fly back overhead. Though first he longs to rejoin them, eventually he stops even noticing when they fly overhead. It may seem that freedom shouldn't feel like death, but a death of some kind needs to happen for the self to fly free once again.

---

In C.S. Lewis's book *The Great Divorce*, men and women in hell take a bus ride to heaven for the day. In heaven they are jolted by the brilliant reality—light so real they have to squint and grass so real it is hard to walk on without wincing.

One of the people from hell comes with a red lizard perched on his shoulder. The lizard whispers into his ears, and sometimes the human tells him to be quiet, while other times the human smiles wickedly. The lizard's name is lust.

An angel comes near and asks the human, "Would you like me to make him quiet?"

"Of course I would," returns the human.

"Then I will kill him," says the angel.

"Oh—ah—look out! You're burning me! Keep away!" retreats the human.

The angel says, "Don't you *want* him killed?"

He responds, "You didn't say anything about *killing* him at first. I hardly meant to bother you with anything so drastic as that."

"It's the only way; shall I kill it?"[25]

Back and forth, the human offers all kinds of excuses—he is not feeling well that day, perhaps he should consult his doctor back home first, and so on—while the angel keeps returning, "May I kill it?"

The human begs, "Why are you torturing me? If you wanted to help me, why didn't you kill the thing without asking me—before I knew? It would be all over by now if you had!"

And the angel says, "I cannot kill it against your will. It is impossible. Have I your permission?"

The human cannot experience both the relief of conquered sin *and* the thrill of lust. It's sin as master, or sin as mastered. It's hell or heaven. It's nothing an angel can decide for him; it's a decision he must make between two mutually exclusive options. Liberation via enslaving sin simply does not exist, and as such it is not one of the options.

Make it personal for yourself. What sins have you by the throat? You may be free to do those sins, but you aren't *free*. What sins have promised you freedom but have only enslaved you to where it's become impossible not to do them when the conditions are right? What sins have deposed you from alive human to Pavlov's dog? What sins are moving you about like pieces on a chessboard, wiping out the things you truly care about? Aren't you tired of what your sin does to you and yours? Don't you long to be free?

If so, then listen to Jesus' words in John 8:34–36:

> Jesus answered them, "Truly, truly, I say to you, everyone who practices sin is a slave to sin. The slave does not remain in the house forever; the son remains forever. So if the Son sets you free, you will be free indeed.

Jesus says if you want to be free, He'll set you free from your sin. Sounds good, right? Yes. Then will you allow Him to kill it?

The freedom of the Herods merely mounts an unpayable debt. At the end of Dave Ramsey's lesson on getting rid of debt, he brings out a pair of scissors and collects the credit cards of people who have just paid their decades-long debts off. And to each "snip, snip," there's a roar of applause from the audience. Even louder, however, are the cheers from the owners of the now-useless cards. Why? Because if you've finally paid off thousands, and you're done with the slavery of debt, you cry out in victory.

If I were to take your sin and cut that up, you'd cry out in pain. But you'd be *free*. Yes, it feels like death. But it's the kind that leads to resurrection. No pair of scissors will do the trick. Neither will resolutions or checklists. But there is a way. It has to do with choosing a different side of the chess board. It's putting yourself in the hands of a different master. You will not be the king or queen. But you will not be a mere pawn either. He doesn't call us pawns. He calls us children—children of God (John 1:12; 1 John 3:1).

And in a universe that has an all-powerful God, it's difficult to imagine a more glorified position for former rebels. So why not start looking for liberation in what isn't slavery?

# CONCLUSION

## Something You Might Not Want That Exists

This is awkward.

You see, it's natural for me to tell funny stories about myself. I like self-deprecating humor. Even if something embarrassing happens to me, I typically see a silver lining because I will have a funny story to tell.

But this is different. This is more like self-deprecating self-deprecation. When I'm completely honest with myself, there are parts of me that drive me crazy. There are characteristics about myself I would change. If I were able to create myself piece-by-piece like they do at Build-A-Bear, the finished product would have been different.

What I'm getting at is that, sometimes, I don't really want *me*.

Yet I very much exist, often a tangle of weaknesses and insecurities and character defects.

There is something in your life that you might not always want, but it too exists. It's *you*.

What I am asking you to believe is that, even if you don't always want yourself—even if you would trade the real version of you for a dozen other versions—you are very much *wanted*. God wanted you to exist. That is why He created you.

*Mirage*

And I'm asking you to believe something more. It's not just that God *wanted* you; it's that God *wants* you. He wants you to be in a relationship with Him. He wants it to be a relationship of knowing and loving, of being known and being loved. He wants *you* in heaven with Him as His child, as His friend.

Do you believe it?

It's difficult trusting that someone can love you completely when that person also knows you completely. If the person knows everything about you and still claims to love you without condition, you are tempted to think there must be a catch. It can be even harder to believe in the unconditional love of God from whom nothing about you is hidden.

---

*The Giver* by Lois Lowry is set in the future.[26] In this futuristic world, there have been enough wars and tragedies that the people in charge feel that they have to dramatically change things. They decide to condition everybody to where society stops *feeling*—as in no emotional depth. There are still words, but no real feelings. There are still disagreements, but no real anger. There is still death, but no sadness. There are still marriages, but no romance. Everyone's very polite to each other, but no love.

There's one twelve-year-old boy who's different from all the others. His name is Jonas. Because Jonas isn't like everybody else, he is chosen for a very special task. He is to become an apprentice to the old, gray-haired "Giver," the only person in the whole city able to feel deeply, both the joys and agonies. The Giver has access to all the memories of the past, and it is these memories that allow the Giver to feel what no one else is able to feel. And now, the Giver is going to give these memories to Jonas, so that eventually Jonas will become the next Giver.

Jonas starts receiving these memories, and he begins to feel what he's never felt before: joy, pain, wonder. He experiences a memory of a family with grandparents and parents and kids, all gathered together in a colorful living room opening presents on Christmas Eve, laughing and enjoying each other's company. It's in this living room memory that Jonas notices a feeling he's never experienced before, something between each person in the room. When he asks the Giver what it was that he sensed in the memory, the Giver gives it a name: "love." *Ah, I like love*, Jonas thinks to himself.

Then Jonas gets really curious about something. He goes home and asks his parents a question that's been bugging him ever since the memory: "Do you love me?"

They laugh and ask if he could be more precise with his language.

He looks confused, so his mother explains, "You could ask, 'Do you enjoy me?' The answer is 'Yes.'"

Then his father speaks up: "Or, 'Do you take pride in my accomplishments?' And the answer is wholeheartedly 'Yes.'"

I think we could understand it if God said to us, "I accept your obedience." I think we could understand it if God said, "I acknowledge your submission." I think we could even under-stand it when God says, "I erase your sins from the record." But you know what we have trouble understanding? It's when God says, "I love you." We have trouble understanding the clearest message in the whole Bible: "For God so loved . . . ."

Somehow, we translate God's "I love you" as, "Now that you're forgiven, you had better get your act together." No. Pause. He loves you. His love doesn't depend on what you have to do. It's about what He's already done which funda-mentally changes who you are.

> But when the fullness of time had come, God sent forth his Son, born of woman, born under the law, to redeem those who were under the law, so that we might receive adoption as sons. And because you are sons, God has sent the Spirit of his Son into our hearts, crying, "Abba! Father!" So you are no longer a slave, but a son, and if a son, then an heir through God (Gal. 4:4–7).

---

I enjoyed the TV series *Monk*, but there was one episode I remember not enjoying at all.[27] Mr. Monk has really bad OCD, which makes him a really good detective. But the OCD renders him typically joyless and uptight and unable to truly connect in relationships. But in this particular episode, Mr. Monk meets an older woman—a really kind, genuinely loving, motherly woman. And there's an instant connection between the two. She had lost her son decades before, and he'd never really had a loving relationship with his mom. So it's really cool: he's often over there for meals, she knits him a scarf, and he begins to experience what it means to be unconditionally loved as a son. This is a big deal for Mr. Monk!

But the OCD starts kicking in. *No one has ever loved me like this with no strings attached*, he reminds himself. *In fact, she's too nice. This has got to be an act. There's got to be a catch.* He starts to think less like a son and more like the detective, until he concocts a solution: She's probably connected to the crime he's trying to solve, and she's trying to get close to him to throw him off. So he starts interrogating her—grilling her—like he would a suspect. She's taken aback. His face gets redder and angrier, because, of course, he's got it all figured out. No one could really love him for who he is. She's a sham. And if she's a sham, she's sure doing a good job pretending to be genuinely hurt by his hostility.

Next thing we know, something happens that's never before happened in a *Monk* episode: Whenever Mr. Monk becomes completely sure about something, he's always right. Not this time. Monk was actually wrong about her being connected to the crime. She was completely innocent. Moreover, Monk was completely wrong about there being a catch. There hadn't been a catch. This lady genuinely loved him as a son. It had been an opportunity for Monk to escape his joyless life of just a bunch of dos and don'ts and to enter into a transformational relationship of love—a love relationship which had started to give him joy. But he got scared, he got cynical, and he checked himself back into his familiar prison cell of loneliness.

As we have seen throughout this book, there are numerous things we might want, but which don't exist. We end the book with something you might not always want, but which definitely exists. It's you. It's not necessarily the version of you which you feel good about letting people see. It's not the résumé version or the smiley church version or the staged social media version. It's you.

Here's the truth about you: God wanted you and that's why He created you. What's more is that God *wants* you. Jesus came to invite you into a transformational relationship of love. To be known and loved completely—that's an invitation which doesn't end in disappointment. Why? It's because it's an invitation into what's really *real*. This is an undying relationship grounded in ultimate reality itself. This is not an uppity deity who stays far off, waiting for us to claw our way through celestial levels to him. Rather, this is a loving God who proved His love by entering history as one of us, dying a cruel death, and rising again to pave the way for us to be brought into a new life of reconciliation and joy. He invites us into an eternity of knowing and loving, of being known and being loved.

It's easy to get cynical hearing about a love which won't peak and plummet based on your performance. But it's there.

Each joy you feel invites you to pursue the source of that joy. In turn, each sorrow you feel invites you to put your trust in something solid which won't buckle and crumble under the weight of your hopes. Joys and sorrows and countless clues in between are God's invitations to trust what's really there: a God who really, truly loves *you*.

Please stop chasing what doesn't exist and allow yourself to be found by the One who does.

# Endnotes

[1] *Gnomeo & Juliet*. Directed by Kelly Asbury. Burbank: Touchstone Pictures, 2011.

[2] *Guardians of the Galaxy*. Directed by James Gunn. Burbank: Marvel Studios, 2014.

[3] *The Lego Movie*. Directed by Christopher Miller and Phil Lord. Burbank: Warner Bros. 2014.

[4] Kaitlyn Alanis, "Kansas Sheriff's Office Said It'd Block All Facebook Access. It 'Created a Monster,'" *The Wichita Eagle*, January 30, 2018, http://www.kansas.com/news/state/article197387119.html (accessed May 17, 2020).

[5] Alan White, "11 Incredibly Powerful Letters from History," *BuzzFeed*, December 9, 2013, https://www.buzzfeed.com/alanwhite/11-incredibly-powerful-hand-written-letters-from-history (accessed May 17, 2020).

[6] Oscar Wilde, *The Picture of Dorian Gray*, ed. Isobel Murray (Oxford: Oxford University Press, 1998).

[7] This is a variation of a joke that can be found on various joke websites. For example, see "A Big Hole in the Ground," https://joek.com/jokes/joke_91.shtml (accessed May 17, 2020).

[8] This is one variation of a joke that can be found on various joke websites. For example, see "Motorcycle Humor," *Northwest Tour and Trail*, May 31, 2004, http://www.blackdogdualsport.com/cycle_humor.htm (accessed May 17, 2020).

⁹ C.S. Lewis, *The Problem of Pain* (San Francisco: HarperSanFrancisco, 2001), 24.

¹⁰ For a fuller discussion of these three ways, see Norman L. Geisler and Daniel J. McCoy, *The Atheist's Fatal Flaw: Exposing Conflicting Beliefs* (Grand Rapids: Baker Books, 2014).

¹¹ Lewis, *Problem of Pain*, 18.

¹² Aldous Huxley, "Chapter Fifteen," *Brave New World*, https://www.huxley.net/bnw/fifteen.html (accessed May 17, 2020).

¹³ *Hook*. Directed by Stephen Spielberg. Universal City: Amblin Entertainment, 1991.

¹⁴ This is a line I first heard from comedian Ken Davis. For more from Ken, see https://www.kendavis.com/.

¹⁵ Or at least "semi-automatic." "Automatic salvation" could be seen as an exaggerative description with regard to the pluralist who believes that, regardless of the religion, there needs to be a transformative effect on the adherent for there to be salvation. Even a universalist (who believes that all people will eventually be saved) might take issue with the word *automatic*, since there is an eventuality and inevitability to the process, not necessarily an automatic suddenness of salvation. "Automatic salvation" is best seen as a description of the pluralist's view of the religions themselves, not necessarily of all people. The obvious implication of this desire would be more (perhaps all) people participating in salvation, regardless of the religion they pursue salvation through.

[16] According to the Bhagavad Gita, Chapter IV, Lord Krishna said, "The fourfold division of castes was created by me according to the apportionment of qualities and duties." See Chapter 4 of the Bhagavad Gita, *Sacred Texts*, https://sacred-texts.com/hin/sbe08/sbe0806.htm (accessed May 17, 2020).

[17] This refers to the deity and demon Mara. See this and other temptations by Mara against the Buddha at Ananda W.P. Guruge, "The Buddha's Encounters with Mara the Tempter: Their Representation in Literature and Art," *Access to Insight*, 2005, https://www.accesstoinsight.org/lib/authors/guruge/wheel419.html (accessed May 17, 2020).

[18] See Sura 2:190 in the Koran.

[19] See 1 Kings 20:43; 21:27; 21:4.

[20] Nicolas Wyatt, "Religion in Ancient Ugarit," in *A Handbook of Ancient Religions*, edited by John R. Hinnells (Cambridge: Cambridge University Press, 2007), 137.

[21] According to a study by the Study of Global Christianity (*Christianity in its Global Context* [South Hamilton: Center for the Study of Global Christianity, 2013], 6), "For the period 1970–2020, several global trends related to religious affiliation are apparent. In 1970, nearly 82% of the world's population was religious. By 2010 this had grown to around 88%, with a projected increase to almost 90% by 2020. Religious adherence is growing largely due to the continuing resurgence of

religion in China. In addition, in 1970 Christianity and Islam represented 48.8% of the global population; by 2020 they will likely represent 57.2%. The global North is becoming more religiously diverse, with more countries becoming home to a greater number of the world's religions. However, religious diversity is decreasing in many countries in the global South with the growth of mainly one religion, most commonly Christianity or Islam."

[22] Saint Augustine, *Confessions*, trans. Henry Chadwick (Oxford: Oxford University Press, 2008), 3.

[23] See "Hear nor Their Sticker," *Tim Hawkins*, https://timhawkins.net/products/hear-nor-their-sticker (accessed May 17, 2020).

[24] *The Stupids*. Directed by John Landis. Beverly Hills: Imagine Entertainment, 1996.

[25] C.S. Lewis, *The Great Divorce* (San Francisco: HarperSanFrancisco, 2001), 106–110.

[26] Lois Lowry, *The Giver* (Boston: Houghton Mifflin Harcourt, 1993).

[27] *Monk*. "Mr. Monk and the Lady Next Door." Season 7, Episode 12. Directed by Tawnia McKiernan. Written by Andy Breckman, Hy Conrad, Joe Toplyn. USA Network. January 23, 2009.

# About the Author

Daniel McCoy is happily married to Susanna, and they have three daughters and two sons. Daniel works as editorial director for Renew.org. He has his bachelor's in theology (Ozark Christian College), his master of arts in apologetics (Veritas International University), and his PhD in theology (North-West University).

He is the co-author of *The Atheist's Fatal Flaw* (Baker, 2014) with Norman Geisler, as well as the general editor of the *Popular Handbook of World Religions* (Harvest House, 2021). His passion is to help people understand that they can totally trust Jesus.